Echoes ll
More Neo-Victorian Poetry

by

JaniceT

ISBN: 1499373279
ISBN-13: 978-1499373271

To Stanley and Emmie

- Index -

Janice T

Introduction

What is Neo-Victorian Poetry? This question became very apparent during my preparation for a public reading of my work in a local cafe. I knew that my approach to that event was amiss, somehow, but it took me some time to realize how. And then it hit me: Would anyone in attendance even know what Neo-Victorian Poetry is? Would they have any familiarity with the Steampunk genre, with which I am loosely affiliated? So, I decided to use that platform as a teaching event, with my poems serving to illustrate the genre, and it worked out perfectly.

Being a Neo-Victorian poet does call for at least some explanation, especially when I am presenting my work outside of a Steampunk venue. For instance, I was not born during the Victorian era; my writing voice is contemporary to the twenty first century. Neo refers to something revived, or modified. Since I write with a modern voice, yet in a Victorian style, I am a Neo-Victorian poet. I write about today while using influences from a long ago yesterday.

As to my Steampunk affiliation, I have loved and appreciated all things Steampunk before it was recognized as a genre. What is Steampunk? Imagine we are living in the late-nineteenth century, (the time of Jules Verne), but are using the technology of today? Would our cell phones be made of copper and run on steam? Verne's flights of scientific and technological fancy inspire such images, and he is considered to be the Father of Steampunk. His imagination has also inspired some of my poems, such as "Jules," however, it is my reliance on metered rhyme that best defines my style of writing.

This is why I claim to be modestly affiliated with the Steampunk genre. Its ambiance resonates with me and feeds me, regardless of which subject I choose. Thus, my poems are about subjects that include airships and steam engines, as well as love, pain, and lessons that I have learned over the years. I sincerely hope that you will gain something of your own from the poems herein.

Enjoy!

Janice T

Echoes II

Janice T

A Better Friend

Though I would play the fool and laugh
And acquiesce at every turn
Without complaint, but to your back,
Nor protest, while my ire burned,
Though I did, out of fear, pretend
I could have been a better friend.

Where dangers loomed and faults I'd see,
With opportunity to say,
No opposition rose in me
To counsel you along the way.
Where I was fearful to offend,
I should have been a better friend.

Had I but loved you as I should
And braved to weather your reply
Intent on guiding where I could
Against the warnings in your eye,
Had my heart charity to spend
I would have been a better friend.

Airship

How far I've flown I neither know nor care.
Much as this open deck my plans are bare.
Of star or compass I have nary need,
But follow as these downy cloud tops lead.

The chilly breezes toying through my hair
Cascade across my skin and jacket flare
While on the bottoms of my booted feet
The engine taps an unrelenting beat.

I acquiesce to gentle bob and sway
Beneath balloon and rigging bloated shape.
Awaiting now the nearly risen sun
I scan the vast expanse and see no one.

And yet, I hear a rumbling of some sort
Then luminescing clouds off to my port
Combusting deep with ever brighter tones
Now booming louder, louder, nearer, NO!

Bombastic airship, cannons bursting now,
Ejected straight at me from out its shroud.
A maniac, that pilot, heaving hard
Just missing our collision by one yard

His tortured face, the horror in those eyes,
For near destroying me, so I surmised,
Until I saw his passing stern ablaze.
Then mammoth winged beast in brutal chase

Janice T

Erupting, fierce and howling, scales agleam.
The hot concussion of its down-spent wing
That final moment as it thrust away
Forced ship and I and all the world to sway.

Then came the screams, the pounding and a moan
As crew and cargo floundered down below
Caught in the violent swinging disarray.
The flaming ship and dragon sped away

To disappear in yet another cloud.
Our vessel's motion finally calmed down.
Those lightly injured put the ship aright.
And unspilled rum was quickly spent that night.

Now star and compass were of urgent need.
This damaged vessel and the injuries
Required that we find a ready port
Equipped to lend us aid of every sort.

I searched in haste upending fore and aft
For sextant, compass, and the proper map,
Then finally we found the guiding star
And made for help that wasn't very far.

By dawn I bid the floating docks goodbye
With only half a crew and resupply
But, now where ere I travel through the sky
I keep the navigation tools nearby.

Antisocial

These uninvited guests
Abrupt and unforeseen
When I was want to rest
Such noisy mirth, they bring

With appetites to quell
From pantry light of means
To entertain as well
Though I would rather dream

Of swaying island palms
And languid lapping sea
But brigands raid my calm
With forced comradery

My strength and larder spent
They amble to the door
Each steals a hug and then
I soon become quite sore

Of endless ardent waves
Through doorway growing closed
And I am soon away
In search of sweet repose

Yet as I now recline
My agitated brain
Spins echoes of the night
To deepen my disdain

Janice T

Till I becalm my mind
And send the echoes forth
But now I find that I'm
Not sleepy anymore.

Echoes II

Janice T

A Rare Day

Sweet comfort breaths into the eaves
Imbuing all who dwell
Within this gentle hostelry
With peaceful ease as well.

A subtle breeze begins to tease
The window's wispy veil
While white waves breach the sunlit beach
And otters ride their swell.

Enveloping and nurturing
Composed to sooth and quell
This all too precious rarity
Consumes me with its spell.

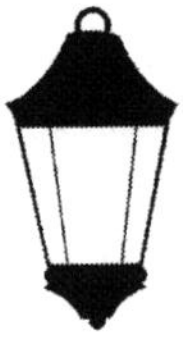

20

Janice T

Blind Rhino

Blind Rhino didn't see the shop display
When through the glass she crashed unfazed unscathed
On through the showering shards she made her way
And woke abruptly in the farthest wall.

Blind Rhino then removed her sleeping shield
From off her eyes and all was soon revealed
She wailed and moaned, collapsing in disgrace
Poor Rhino. You and I share common traits.

Janice T

Caged Heart

If my heart were not caged,
Within this bosom bound,
It would then be at liberty
To follow you around.
But, lacking lips to kiss
And arms to hold you tight
This heart must stay right where it is
No matter how it fights
To be with you.

Janice T

Coconuts

Fifteen thousand coconuts
Fell on a dead man's head
And why he lay there no one know
Till suddenly he said,
"Why pound me so with coconuts?
Just what do you expect?"
He then got up, wiped off his dirty
Arms and legs and left.

Janice T

Coffee

It is the aroma I sense first
When thinking just to quench my thirst
And then the warmth that permeates
The cup as I start to partake
The steaming sensuous delight
Of jungles glistening in the night
Of wild abounding living things
That have their essence in the beans
Which, roasted, ground, and brewed with care
Transport me to some distant lair
And I am quenched of many thirsts
But it's the aroma I sensed first.

Janice T

Dreamer

Encapsulated by her thoughts
Beyond all access for a time
She only knows to thus compose
The shapes and colors of her mind.

From fertile regions deep within
They sprout and grow a living vine
And cradling they comfort bring
These shapes and colors of her mind.

Though she disrobes this furtive realm
To leave it languishing behind
She can't completely ever flee
The shapes and colors of her mind.

Drums of Doom

The drums of doom were beating
To a mammoth iron hammer
Rising bulging, brutish muscle
Pulling down through smoke and cinders
Metal bursting under metal
Straining up behemoth hammer
Through exploding, white-hot splinters
Slow the rhythmed, pounding manner
Of that massive iron hammer.

The drums of doom were beating
At the heart of every creature
Mad with panic of destruction
Birds flew blindly at each other
Barking dogs ran brisk, tight circles
Every living beast berserking
All humanity lunged sprawling
Into tunnels, basements, shelters
There to sit and wait and swelter.

The drums of doom were beating
In the minds of each world leader
Grabbing up their wives and babies
Racing down through miles of strata
To their special, lead-lined bunkers
Miles beneath exploding buildings
Bursting bodies, death and dying
Well below dark devastation
Sat the leaders of each nation.

Janice T

The drums of doom were beating
With a cadence deep with whispers
Over scorched, distorted valleys
Sheltered cities blasted level
Crimson oceans, lakes and rivers
Clouds of vapor, smoke and ashes
Streaming piles of flash-baked bodies
Over everything remaining
Rolled the pounding-low, sustaining.

The drums of doom were beating
And depleting every bunker
Slowly, up through narrow channels
Up past levels of striation
Came the leaders, wives, and children
Towards a strangely filtered sunlight
Through the portals gaping open
Into air mixed thick with ashes
And a world in frozen chaos.

The drums of doom were beating
Growing louder, quicker, louder
Setting countless ghosts to marching
Steady motion coming faster
Closing in on gaping portals
Terror rending at each leader
Plunging back into their bunkers
Wives and children, screaming, followed
Down into their lead-lined hollows

Echoes II

The drums of doom were beating
At the door of each deep shelter
Closed and locked to block the horror
Knocking to a constant rhythm
Ever sounding, pounding, hounding
Air drew thin in heavy breathing
Soon a last slow breath depleting
And the drums of doom stopped beating.

Janice T

Echoes II

Janice T

Each Morning

Each morning when I wake to see
You by my side, sweet slumbering
I say a prayer that I might be
A better wife to you.

Each day I hunger but to know
That you are happy 'ere you go
That I'll be, when you venture home,
A better wife to you.

Each night I long with you to lay
In sweet repose at end of day,
Your love, your sweetheart, and I pray,
A better wife to you.

Engulfed

She loved the fairy touch of fog
That kissed her as she hastened home
With bundles in her swinging hands
Her focus on the open tome

Left waiting on her heated stove
To one ambrosial recipe.
Distracted from her sprightly steps
It hovers in her memory.

Now as she goes she starts to nose
The fragrance of her lambent hearth
And hurries ever faster on
Encouraged by it's promised warmth.

She muses on the woven throw
Tossed carelessly on her divan
That sits entire before the fire
And that's where her unease began

Oh, she could sense the fog grow dense
With humors never known of fog,
Sees woven throw too near the flame
Of bursting bright combusting log

The oven, hot, and hotter still
Her book igniting on the stove.
As horror gripped her very heart.
She had to see, she had to know

Janice T

So stirs to running quick and smart
As bundles from her loosed hands flew
Well out to burst upon the ground
And thicker grew the acrid fumes.

With slowing step, with heaving breath,
She blindly searches for her door
Then starts to pull her raven hair
For there was smoke, and nothing more.

Two phantom hands take hold of hers
To pry them from her tortured scalp.
She searches blindly, then perceives
A figure, eyes, and moving mouth,

Then seems to hear, though distantly,
The voicing of an earnest plea
Which pulls her gently from the haze
Dispelling ambiguity

As vapors softly melt away
Her fists now cradled in his hands
She searches through his anxious eyes
With all her will she steals a glance

To either side and, round about
Quite disbelieving what she sees
Or smells, for now the mist is gone,
And all is as it ought to be.

Echoes II

Her heart, though pounding in her breast,
Works hard to slow and then to ease
As quivers echo through her breath
And she succumbs to gravity

But no, he holds her in his arms
This man who was but walking near
When panicked wails, his ears beheld,
Of potent, agonizing fear.

He rights her then, as best he can
As from brief stupor she awakes
To find her form so gently born
Within a journeyman's embrace

As evidenced of tools and kit
That lay well scattered at their feet.
Which he dismisses with a wave
And as she stands more steadily

He tentatively pulls away,
Retrieves his things, then follows her
To where the castoff parcels lay
Intact. Not one of them has burst.

Ashamed, confused, she tries to flee
But he has seen these signs before
So stalls her bid to run away
And sweetly, gently he implores

Janice T

Her patience while he takes her hands,
Examines them, then softly sighs,
For on her skin, opaque and thin,
The evidence of burns reside.

And as she jerks her hands away
He lifts his shirt up to reveal
A massive scar, much worse by far
And says he knows just how she feels.

Relief brings laughter to their lips,
Brief introductions following,
Then past his frame, not far away,
Her little cottage she could see

She shyly asks that he partake
A home-cooked meal, as recompense,
To which he gratefully agrees.
And he's been with her ever since.

Echoes II

Janice T

Gossip

Their words are laced with lies and haste.
Beware, for gossipers have come
With vile agenda to create
Opinion when some deed is done.

And subtly their sorcery
Compels both history and fact
To shift and bend as they intend,
Conforming with their selfish pact.

Beware, for with their siren call
They lure sweet Justice to the rocks
Where they can feed upon despair
And brutalize the overwrought.

Janice T

Heart Aflame

That day when I first met him
Quite unexpectedly
I saw a little something
That lit a spark in me.

This curious sensation
Combusted with desire
From embers softly glowing
Till now it is a pyre

Which nothing can extinguish
Because he does his part
Of ever always fanning
This flame within my heart.

Janice T

Intangibles

This gaping wallet in my hand
so fully spent not coin remains
and oh how sweet the where and when
continue still to sustain.

Such artifacts that I collect
serve but to jog at memory
which shelters, clear of moth or dust
or rust, in what is yet me.

A lust for mansions, vessels, cars,
for pockets bulging ready cash,
the pace and ease of luxury,
once held me, meat in it's grasp.

Now, victim of commercial gain
abandoned by the banker's dole
I am reborn, I disobey,
and burn the road as I go.

Janice T

Jules

Nibbed pen in hand, he labored on an open page.
In truth, his eyes were focused down upon the moon,
Volcanoes spewing as his capsule glided by.
An interruption shocked him back into his room.

He spied the page before him taking careful note
Before addressing matters that were near at hand.
The noontime meal was ready, calling him away
Still wondering if he and his passengers could land.

No sedentary figure, he had traveled well
And far beyond the borders of his writing desk
To scour oceans deep for all that man could need,
Or delve into strange doings in cavernous depths.

He lived upon an island quite mysterious,
For eighty days he roamed our orb by land and sea
The very center of the Earth he once explored
And on comet he lived, accidentally.

He even sailed to Africa in his balloon.
An Arctic summer ocean he made manifest.
So many wondrous tales of traveling had he,
And all seen through the pages on his writing desk.

Knuckle-Draggers

This hamlet long has been my home
A place to grow and thrive
A thing of sweet vitality
With promise as its guide.

But now I fear, these past few years,
A creature has arrived,
A beastial thing of habits mean
That slithers in at night.

It's hallmark is immodesty
In every sordid hue
And lurid vice, at any price,
Displayed in open view.

If only they were fleeing from
Encampments of despair
To be renewed, and thus imbued
With manners soft and fair,

But each is bred of discontent
And this they blindly breed
Who wallow deep in drugs and drink
And raucous revelry

Would that the portals, gaping wide,
Which cater to their lusts
Could be transformed into the form
Of what this town once was:

Janice T

A quaint abode, of honor honed,
A place to grow and thrive
A thing of sweet vitality
With promise as it's guide.

My Heart Blooms

The day was young and sweet and fair
When suddenly you came
Upon a garden in neglect
While strolling down a lane,

And in a disused corner there
Where weed and drought consume
You found, upon a slender stem,
A melancholy bloom.

With deftness and a careful eye
You dredged the meager ground
But all the root was withered,
Every tendril dry and brown.

Yet, tenderly you cradled it
And, hastening, made home,
Excising root you placed the shoot
Within a vase well blown.

Then down that throat a liquor sweet
And tepid did you pour,
You waited and you waited
For the plant to take the cure.

Exhausted, spent, assailed, you slept,
But through a lucid haze
You thought you saw the liquid drop
And leaf and flower raise.

Janice T

A morning ray betokened day
And there within the glass
A single rose, of grace composed,
Blossomed, and all surpass.

The day is young and sweet and fair
That rose was I, you see.
And my heart blooms with love for you
Who deigned to rescue me.

Janice T

Ode to an Imp

Sometimes the imp is resident
In silly things you say and do,
Yet always are such antics meant
To entertain and lift my mood.

This aspect of your nature, spent
So sweetly, though I seem unmoved,
In truth persuades me to relent
And does endear me so to you.

It is a gift that you present
When I see everything eskew
And I am ever in your debt
For silly things you say and do.

Janice T

On Hope

The most essential scope of hope
Is that the door is still ajar
Not neatly closed, as some suppose,
Nor by forced obligation barred.
Though some cut short the sweet report
Of promise there are those who see
A glimmer through the portal yet
Of that which hope portents to be.

Janice T

Portals

Portals loom in every life:
Directions that define our walk.
Some are primed to open wide
And others mercifully locked.

Wise are we who learn to leave
Alone the door that will not give,
Appreciating, too, that each
Is fitted with a knob and hinge.

But woe to we who pull and plead
And force the way when we should not,
Or else begrudgingly proceed
In disillusionment and want

It is our need to test and try,
To grope and grow – it is our lot,
Thus, some are primed to open wide
And some are mercifully locked.

Janice T

Promised

Her future had been chiseled out in stone
With every instance as it ought to be,
As was the manner of the ancient code,
The breeding template of her family.

She bowed to this much like a wilting rose,
A brilliant blossom bled of vibrancy,
And nothing in her manner or her tone
Gave any quotient of her misery.

And through it all she had a stranglehold,
As did so many in her ancestry,
On one great promise someone had foretold
In otherwise neglected prophecy:

One day, somehow, a bride would break the mold,
Would get to live her life fulfilled and free,
And like the others born into her fold
She watched and waited, hoping it was she.

Echoes II

Janice T

Q & A: Rules

Q:

Oh, Classic Verse, it seems a curse
Has long consumed your heart
With rules on rhyme and time, and worse:
To confiscate your art.
Why bow you so to what you know
To be but a cheap device?
Let thoughts unfold, be uncontrolled,
And fluid form suffice.

A:

Ah, but you see, in verse I'm free
To work within the lines
Which censor ambiguity
And elevate my rhymes
To rhythmed regularity
In balanced, toned array
So I can treat upon the meat
Of what I want to say.

Janice T

Reverberations

These dulcet tones that echo through
The chambers of my heart
Have origin in every sigh
And whisper you impart
Into the very channels of
My close and waiting ears
Reverberating, gentle things
They vanquish all I fear
Till I concede to chorusing
With murmurs shy of hum
And we together sweetly sing
In resonance as one.

Echoes II

Janice T

S. F. Marina

A song is on the lips of distant
ships that pass this foggy night
attuned to every sleeping vessel moored
each lapping breath of tide.

My back now to the sea
my elbows resting on the metal rails
I stare across the vacant, misty street
and into other realms

of cathode ray tubes each a different
hue set into blank face stone
displaying pantomimes of varied kinds
in each and every home.

I lean there changing channels at a
glance until I chance to see
someone standing in a distant
window staring back at me.

Toxic

I grow fat astride the carcass of regret
Feast well upon self-pity and despair
So bloated now, unable to forget
Derisive apparitions everywhere

Absorbing every thought, my ire spent
Each waking moment, every dream a dare
To trust in none and never to repent
This cloying cloak of martyrdom I wear

To lavishly engorge in dense caress
Consuming while consumed my only care
As bulk and tonnage bloat past full extent
And screaming seams take all that they can bear

Of tortured fabric, bulging, bursting wet
Unbridled torrent surging, slowing, spare,
Collapsing into limpid, shuddered breath.
In sweet exhaustion, prone and cold and bare

As toxic whispers echo my lament
Which at my labored heart yet will to tear
Though subtle variations of intent
Come wafting into view in graceful air

To intertwine, with reason intersect,
Till every livid cue is hanging where
At length, perceiving that the true neglect
Was misassigned? No! It was I who erred

Janice T

The onus, squarely mine, oh grievous blame
That tunes my tears unto a new lament
Beseeching mercy for what I became
But oh how sweet that carcass of regret.

Echoes II

Janice T

Two Stones

Sweet flowers grew, and grasses blew,
About a pretty garden stone,
While on a rough and wooded bluff,
A piece of granite lay alone.

The comely stone was rightly owned
By one of gentle, fragile hand.
The other, gleaned and brusquely cleaned,
Sat in a palm it could not span.

Then came a morn of promise born
A chamber opened, both went in,
Yet, while they froze in brief repose,
The vessel soon commenced to spin.

At first, in unison they rolled,
But out of sync, the tears began,
Transforming bed and bond, and all
To loosely saturated sand.

Then brief, colliding, bashing hurts
Gave way to blissful harmony
And through each turn, from fight to friend,
They both were altered, subtly.

All jagged edges slowly smoothed,
And more than not gave sweet caress.
No longer coarse, disparate stones
But precious, polished, mated gems.

Echoes II

Janice T

~~ Thank you ~~

If you are interested in finding more information about the poetry of JaniceT, visit her blog at:
http://janice-t.weebly.com

Also available:
Echoes: Neo-Victorian Poetry (2013)

60403468R00045

Made in the USA
Charleston, SC
31 August 2016